D0815186

the anabaptist vision

BY HAROLD S. BENDER

HERALD PRESS
Scottdale, Pennsylvania
Kitchener, Ontario

20 19 18 17 16 15 14 13 12 11 10 9 8

THE ANABAPTIST VISION[1]

"Judged by the reception it met at the hands of those in power, both in Church and State, equally in Roman Catholic and in Protestant countries, the Anabaptist movement was one of the most tragic in the history of Christianity; but, judged by the principles, which were put into play by the men who bore this reproachful nickname, it must be pronounced one of the most momentous and significant undertakings in man's eventful religious struggle after the truth. It gathered up the gains of earlier movements, it is the spiritual soil out of which all nonconformist sects have sprung, and it is the first plain announcement in modern history of a programme for a new type of Christian society which the modern world, especially in America and England, has been slowly realizing — an absolutely free and independent religious society, and a State in which every man counts as a man, and has his share in shaping both Church and State."

These words of Rufus M. Jones[2] constitute one of the best characterizations of Anabaptism and its contribution to our modern Christian culture to be found in the English language. They were brave words when they were written thirty-five years ago, but they have been abundantly verified by a generation of Anabaptist research since that time.[3] There can be no question but that the great principles of freedom of conscience, separation of church and state, and voluntarism in religion, so basic in American Protestantism and so essential to democracy, ultimately are derived from the Anabaptists of the Reformation period, who for the first time clearly enunciated them and challenged the Christian world to follow them in practice. The line of descent through the centuries since that time may not always be clear, and may have passed through other intermediate movements and groups, but the debt to original Anabaptism is unquestioned.

The sixteenth-century reformers understood the Anabaptist position on this point all too well, and deliberately rejected it. The best witness is Heinrich Bullinger, Zwingli's successor in Zurich, whose active life-span covers the first fifty years of the history of the Swiss Anabaptists and who knew them so well that he published two extensive treatises against them in 1531 and 1561. According to Bullinger, the Swiss Brethren taught that:

One cannot and should not use force to compel anyone to accept the faith, for faith is a free gift of God. It is wrong to compel anyone by force or coercion to embrace the faith, or to put to death anyone for the sake of his erring faith. It is an error that in the church any sword other than that of

4

the divine Word should be used. The secular kingdom should be separated from the church, and no secular ruler should exercise authority in the church. The Lord has commanded simply to preach the Gospel, not to compel anyone by force to accept it. The true church of Christ has the characteristic that it suffers and endures persecution but does not inflict persecution upon anyone.[4]

Bullinger reports these ideas, not in commendation but in condemnation urging the need of rigid suppression. He attempts a point by point refutation of the Anabaptist teaching, closing with the assertion that to put to death Anabaptists is a necessary and commendable service.

But great as is the Anabaptist contribution to the development of religious liberty, this concept not only does not exhaust but actually fails to define the true essence of Anabaptism. In the last analysis freedom of religion is a purely formal concept, barren of content; it says nothing about the faith or the way of life of those who advocate it, nor does it reveal their goals or program of action. And Anabaptism had not only clearly defined goals but also an action program of definiteness and power. In fact the more intimately one becomes acquainted with this group the more one becomes conscious of the great vision that shaped their course in history and for which they gladly gave their lives.

Before describing this vision it is well to note its attractiveness to the masses of Christians of the sixteenth century. Sebastian Franck, himself an opponent, wrote in 1531, scarcely seven years after the rise of the movement in Zurich:

The Anabaptists spread so rapidly that their teaching soon covered the land as it were. They soon gained a large following, and baptized thousands, drawing to themselves many sincere souls who had a zeal for God. . . . They increased so rapidly that the world feared an uprising by them though I have learned that this fear had no justification whatsoever.[5]

In the same year Bullinger wrote that "the people were running after them as though they were living saints."[6] Another contemporary writer asserts that "Anabaptism spread with such speed that there was reason to fear that the majority of the common people would unite with this sect."[7] Zwingli was so frightened by the power of the movement that he complained that the struggle with the Catholic party was "but child's play" compared to the conflict with the Anabaptists.[8]

The dreadful severity of the persecution of the Anabaptist movement in the years 1527-60 not only in Switzerland, South Germany, and Thuringia, but in all the Austrian lands as well as in the Low Countries, testifies to the power of the movement and the desperate haste with which Catholic, Lutheran, and Zwinglian authorities alike strove to throttle it before it should be too late. The notorious decree issued in 1529 by the Diet of Spires (the same diet which protested the restriction of evangelical liberties) summarily passed the sentence of death upon all Anabaptists, ordering that "every Anabaptist and rebaptized person of either sex should be put to death by fire, sword, or some other way."[9] Repeatedly in subsequent sessions of the imperial diet this decree was reinvoked and intensified; and as late as 1551 the Diet of Augsburg issued a decree ordering that judges and jurors who had scruples against pronouncing the death sentence on Anabaptists be removed from office and punished by heavy fines and imprisonment.

The authorities had great difficulty in executing their program of suppression, for they soon discovered that the Anabaptists feared neither torture nor death, and gladly sealed their faith with their blood. In fact the joyful testimony of the Anabaptist martyrs was a great stimulus to new recruits, for it stirred the imagination of the populace as nothing else could have done.

Finding, therefore, that the customary method of individual trials and sentences was proving totally inadequate to stem the tide, the authorities resorted to the desperate expedient of sending out through the land companies of armed executioners and mounted soldiers to hunt down the Anabaptists and kill them on the spot singly or *en masse* without trial or sentence. The most atrocious application of this policy was made in Swabia where the original 400 special police of 1528 sent against the Anabaptists proved too small a force and had to be increased to 1,000. An imperial provost marshal, Berthold Aichele, served as chief administrator of this bloody program in Swabia and other regions until he finally broke down in terror and dismay, and after an execution at Brixen lifted his hands to heaven and swore a solemn oath never again to put to death an Anabaptist, which vow he kept.[10] The Count of Alzey in the Palatinate, after 350 Anabaptists had been executed there, was heard to exclaim, "What shall I do, the more I kill, the greater becomes their number!"

The extensive persecution and martyrdom of the Anabaptists testify not only of the great extent of the movement but also of the power of the vision that burned within them. This is most effectively presented in a moving account written in 1542 and taken from the ancient Hutterian chronicle where it is found at the close of a report of 2,173 brethren and sisters who gave their lives for their faith.[11]

No human being was able to take away out of their hearts what they had experienced, such zeal-

8

ous lovers of God were they. The fire of God burned within them. They would die the bitterest death, yea, they would die ten deaths rather than forsake the divine truth which they had espoused. . . .

They had drunk of the waters which had flowed from God's sanctuary, yea, the water of life. They realized that God helped them to bear the cross and to overcome the bitterness of death. The fire of God burned within them. Their tent they had pitched not here upon earth, but in eternity, and of their faith they had a foundation and assurance. Their faith blossomed as a lily, their loyalty as a rose, their piety and sincerity as the flower of the garden of God. The angel of the Lord battled for them that they could not be deprived of the helmet of salvation. Therefore they bore all torture and agony without fear. The things of this world they counted in their holy mind only as shadows, having the assurance of greater things. They were so drawn unto God that they knew nothing, sought nothing, desired nothing, loved nothing but God alone. Therefore they had more patience in their suffering than their enemies in tormenting them.

. . . The persecutors thought they could dampen and extinguish the fire of God. But the prisoners sang in their prisons and rejoiced so that the enemies outside became much more fearful than the prisoners and did not know what to do with them. . . .

Many were talked to in wonderful ways, often day and night. They were argued with, with great cunning and cleverness, with many sweet and smooth words, by monks and priests, by doctors of theology, with much false testimony, with threats and scolding and mockery, yea, with lies and grievous slander against the brotherhood, but none of these things moved them or made them falter.

From the shedding of such innocent blood arose Christians everywhere, brothers all, for all this persecution did not take place without fruit. . . .

Perhaps this interpretation of the Anabaptist spirit should be discounted as too glowing, coming as it does from the group itself, but certainly it is nearer to the truth than the typical harsh nineteenth-century interpretation of the movement which is well represented by the opening sentence of *Ursula*, the notable historical novel on the Anabaptists published in 1878 by the Swiss Gottfried Keller, next to Goethe perhaps the greatest of all writers in the German language:

Times of religious change are like times when the mountains open up; for then not only do all the marvelous creatures of the human spirit come forth, the great golden dragons, magic beings and crystal spirits, but there also come to light all the hateful vermin of humanity, the host of rats and mice and pestiferous creation, and so it was at the time of the Reformation in the northeast part of Switzerland. [12]

Before defining the Anabaptist vision, it is essential to state clearly who is meant by the term "Anabaptist," since the name has come to be used in modern historiography to cover a wide variety of Reformation groups, sometimes thought of as the whole "left wing of the Reformation" (Roland Bainton), "the Bolsheviks of the Reformation" (Preserved Smith). Although the definitive history of Anabaptism has not yet been written, we know enough today to draw a clear line of demarcation between original evangelical and constructive Anabaptism on the one hand, which was born in the bosom of Zwinglianism in Zurich, Switzerland, in 1525, and established in the Low Countries in 1533, and the various mystical, spiritualistic, revolutionary, or even antinomian related and unrelated groups on the other hand, which came and went like the flowers of the field in those days of the great renovation. The former, Anabaptism proper, maintained an unbroken course in Switzerland, South Germany, Austria, and Holland throughout the sixteenth century, and has continued until the present day in the Mennonite movement, now almost 500,000 baptized members strong in Europe and America.[13] There is no longer any excuse for permitting our understanding of the distinct character of this genuine Anabaptism to be obscured by Thomas Müntzer and the Peasants War, the Münsterites, or any other aberration of Protestantism in the sixteen century.

There may be some excuse, however, for a failure on the part of the uninformed student to see clearly what the Anabaptist vision was, because of the varying interpretations placed upon the movement even by those who mean to appreciate and approve it. There are, for instance, the socialist writers, led by Kautsky, who would make Anabaptism either "the forerunner of the modern socialism" or the "culminating effort of medieval communism," and who in reality see it only as the external religious shell of a class movement.[14] There are the sociologists with their partial socio-economic determinism as reflected in Richard Niebuhr's approach to the social origin of religious denominations. There is Albert Ritschl, who sees in Anabaptism an ascetic semi-monastic continuation of the medieval Franciscan tertiaries, and locates the seventeenth-century Pietists in the same line;[15] and Ludwig Keller, who finds Anabaptists throughout the pre-Reformation period in the guise of Waldenses and other similar groups whom he chooses to call "the old-evangelical brotherhood,"[16] and for whom he posits a continuity from earliest times. Related to Keller are the earlier Baptist historians (and certain Mennonites) who rejoice to find in the Anabaptists the missing link which keeps them in the apostolic succession of the true church back through the Waldenses, Bogomils, Cathari, Paulicians, and Donatists, to Pentecost. More recently there is Rufus M. Jones who is inclined to class the Anabaptists with the mystics, and Walter Koehler who finds an Erasmian humanist origin for them.

However, there is another line of interpretation, now almost 100 years old, which is being increasingly accepted and which is probably destined to dominate the field. It is the one which holds that Anabaptism is the culmination of the Reformation, the fulfillment of the original vision of Luther and Zwingli, and thus makes it a consistent evangelical Protestantism seeking to recreate without compromise the original New Testament church, the vision of Christ and the apostles. This line of interpretation begins in 1848 with Max Göbel's great *Geschichte des christlichen Lebens in der Rheinisch-Westfälischen Kirche*, continues with the epoch-making work of C. A. Cornelius, particularly in his *Geschichte des Münsterschen Aufruhrs* (1855-1860), follows in the work of men like Johann Loserth, Karl Rembert, and John Horsch, and is represented by such contemporaries as Ernst Correll of Washington and Fritz Blanke of Zurich. A quotation from Göbel may serve to illustrate this interpretation:

The essential and distinguishing characteristic of this church is its great emphasis upon the actual personal conversion and regeneration of every Christian through the Holy Spirit. . . . They aimed with special emphasis at carrying out and realizing the Christian doctrine and faith in the heart and life of every Christian in the whole Christian church. Their aim was the bringing together of all the true believers out of the great degenerated

13

national churches into a true Christian church. That which the Reformation was originally intended to accomplish they aimed to bring into full immediate realization. [17]

And Johann Loserth says:

More radically than any other party for church reformation the Anabaptists strove to follow the footsteps of the church of the first century and to renew unadulterated original Christianity. [18]

The evidence in support of this interpretation is overwhelming, and can be taken from the statements of the contemporary opponents of the Anabaptists as well as from the Anabaptists themselves. Conrad Grebel, the founder of the Swiss Brethren movement, states clearly this point of view in his letter to Thomas Müntzer of 1524, in words written on behalf of the entire group which constitute in effect the original Anabaptist pronunciamento:

Just as our forebears [the Roman Catholic Papal Church] fell away from the true God and the knowledge of Jesus Christ and of the right faith in him, and from the one true, common divine word, from the divine institutions, from Christian love and life, and lived without God's law and gospel in human, useless, un-Christian customs and ceremonies, and expected to attain salvation therein, yet fell far short of it, as the evangelical preachers [Luther, Zwingli, etc.] have declared, and to some extent are still declaring; so today, too, every man wants to be saved by superficial faith, without fruits of faith, without the baptism of test and probation, without love and hope, without right Christian practices, and wants to persist in all the old fashion of personal vices, and in the common ritualistic and anti-Christian customs of baptism and of the Lord's Supper, in disrespect for the divine word and in respect for the word of the pope and of the antipapal preachers, which yet is not equal to the divine word nor in harmony with it. In respecting persons and in manifold seduction there is grosser and more pernicious error now than ever has been since the beginning of the world. In the same error we, too, lingered as long as we heard and read only the evangelical preachers who are to blame for all this, in punishment for our sins. But after we took the Scriptures in hand, too, and consulted it on many points, we have been instructed somewhat and have discovered the great and hurtful error of the shepherds, of ours too, namely that we do not daily beseech God earnestly with constant groanings to be brought out of this destruction of all godly life and out of human abominations, and to attain to true faith and divine instruction.[19]

A similar statement was made in 1538, after fourteen years of persecution, by an Anabaptist leader who spoke on behalf on his group in the great colloquy at Berne with the leaders of the Reformed Church:

While yet in the national church, we obtained much instruction from the writings of Luther, Zwingli, and others, concerning the mass and other papal ceremonies, that they are vain. Yet we recognized a great lack as regards repentance, conversion, and the true Christian life. Upon these things my mind was bent. I waited and hoped for a year or two, since the minister had much to say of amendment of life, of giving to the poor, loving one another, and abstaining from evil. But I could not close my eyes to the fact that the doctrine which was preached and which was based on the Word of God, was not carried out. No beginning was made toward true Christian living, and there was no unison in the teaching concerning the things that were necessary. And although the mass and the images were finally abolished, true repentance and Christian love were not in evidence. Changes were made only as concerned external things. This gave me occasion to inquire further into these matters. Then God sent His messengers, Conrad Grebel and others, with whom I conferred about the fundamental teachings of the apostles and the Christian life and practice. I found them men who had surrendered themselves to the doctrine of Christ by "Bussfertigkeit" [repentance evidenced by fruits]. With their assistance we established a congregation in which repentance was in evidence by newness of life in Christ.[20]

It is evident from these statements that the Anabaptists were concerned most of all about "a true Christian life," that is, a life patterned after the teaching and example of Christ. The reformers, they believed, whatever their profession may have been, did not secure among the people true repentance, regeneration, and Christian living as a result of their preaching. The Reformation emphasis on faith was good but inadequate, for without newness of life, they held, faith is hypocritical.

This Anabaptist critique of the Reformation was a sharp one, but it was not unfair. There is abundant evidence that although the original goal sought by Luther and Zwingli was "an earnest Christianity" for all, the actual outcome was far less, for the level of Christian living among the Protestant population was frequently lower than it had been before under Catholicism. Luther himself was keenly conscious of the deficiency. In April 1522 he expressed the hope that, "We who at the present are well nigh heathen under a Christian name, may yet organize a Christian assembly."[21] In December 1525 he had an important conversation with Caspar Schwenckfeld, concerning the establishment of the New Testament church. Schwenckfeld pointed out that the establishment of the new church had failed to result in spiritual and moral betterment of the people, a fact which Luther admitted, for Schwenckfeld states that "Luther regretted very much that no amendment of life was in evidence."[22] Between 1522 and 1527 Luther repeatedly mentioned his concern to establish a true Christian church, and his desire to provide for earnest Christians (*"Die mit Ernst Christen sein wollen"*) who would confess the gospel with their lives as well as with their tongues. He thought of entering the names of these "earnest Christians" in a special book and having them meet separately from the mass of nominal Christians, but concluding that he would not have sufficient of such people, he dropped the plan.[22 a] Zwingli faced the same problem; he was in fact specifically challenged by the Swiss Brethren to set up such a church; but he refused and followed Luther's course.[23] Both reformers decided that it was better to include the masses within the fold of the church than to form a fellowship of true Christians only. Both certainly expected the preaching of the Word and the ministration of the sacraments to bear fruit in an earnest Christian life, at least among some, but they reckoned with a permanently large and indifferent mass. In taking this course, said the Anabaptists, the reformers surrendered their original purpose, and abandoned the divine intention. Others may say that they were wise and statesmanlike leaders.[24]

The Anabaptists, however, retained the original vision of Luther and Zwingli, enlarged it, gave it body and form, and set out to achieve it in actual experience. They proceeded to organize a church composed solely of earnest Christians, and actually found the people for it. They did not believe in any case that the size of the response should determine whether or not the truth of God should be applied, and they refused to compromise. They preferred to make a radical break with 1,500 years of history and culture if necessary rather than to break with the New Testament.

May it not be said that the decision of Luther and Zwingli to surrender their original vision was the tragic turning point of the Reformation? Professor Karl Mueller, one of the keenest and fairest interpreters of the Refmation, evidently thinks so, for he says, "The aggressive, conquering power, which Lutheranism manifested in its first period was lost everywhere at the moment when the governments took matters in hand and established the Lutheran Creed,"[25] that is to say, when Luther's mass church concept was put into practice. Luther in his later years expressed disappointment at the final outcome of the Reformation, stating that the people had become more and more indifferent toward religion and the moral outlook was more deplorable than ever. His last years were embittered by the consciousness of partial failure, and his expressions of dejection are well known. Contrast this sense of defeat at the end of Luther's outwardly successful career with the sense of victory in the hearts of the Anabaptist martyrs who laid down their lives in what the world would call defeat, conscious of having kept faith with their vision to the end.

Having defined genuine Anabaptism in its Reformation setting, we are ready to examine its central teachings. The Anabaptist vision included three major points of emphasis; first, a new conception of the essence of Christianity as discipleship; second, a new conception of the church as a brotherhood; and third, a new ethic of love and nonresistance. We turn now to an exposition of these points.

First and fundamental in the Anabaptist vision was the conception of the essence of Christianity as discipleship. It was a concept which meant the transformation of the entire way of life of the individual believer and of society so that it should be fashioned after the teachings and example of Christ.[26] The Anabaptists could not understand a Christianity which made regeneration, holiness, and love primarily a matter of intellect, of doctrinal belief, or of subjective ".experience," rather than one of the transformation of life. They demanded an outward expression of the inner experience. Repentance must be "evidenced" by newness of behavior. "In evidence" is the keynote which rings through the testimonies and challenges of the early Swiss Brethren when they are called to give an account of themselves. The whole life was to be brought literally under the lordship of Christ in a covenant of discipleship, a covenant which the Anabaptist writers delighted to emphasize.[27] The focus of the

Christian life was to be not so much the inward experience of the grace of God, as it was for Luther, but the outward application of that grace to all human conduct and the consequent Christianization of all human relationships. The true test of the Christian, they held, is discipleship. The great word of the Anabaptists was not "faith" as it was with the reformers, but "following" (*nachfolge Christi*). And baptism, the greatest of Christian symbols, was accordingly to be for them the "covenant of a good conscience toward God" (1 Peter 3:21),[28] the pledge of a complete commitment to obey Christ, and not primarily the symbol of a past experience. The Anabaptists had faith, indeed, but they used it to produce a life. Theology was for them a means, not an end.

That the Anabaptists not only proclaimed the ideal of full Christian discipleship but achieved, in the eyes of their contemporaries and even of their opponents, a measurably higher level of performance than the average, is fully witnessed by the sources. The early Swiss and South German reformers were keenly aware of this achievement and its attractive power. Zwingli knew it best of all, but Bullinger, Capito, Vadian, and many others confirm his judgment that the Anabaptist Brethren were unusually sincere, devoted, and effective Christians. However, since the Brethren refused to accept the state church system which the reformers were building, and in addition made "radical" demands which might have changed the entire social order, the leaders of the Reformation were completely baffled in their understanding of the movement, and professed to believe that the Anabaptists were hypocrites of the darkest dye. Bullinger, for instance, calls them "devilish enemies and destroyers of the Church of God."[29] Nevertheless they had to admit the apparent superiority of their life. In Zwingli's last book against the Swiss Brethren (1527), for instance, the following is found:

If you investigate their life and conduct, it seems at first contact irreproachable, pious, unassuming, attractive, yea, above this world. Even those who are inclined to be critical will say that their lives are excellent.[30]

Bullinger, himself, who wrote bitter diatribes against them, was compelled to admit of the early Swiss Brethren that

Those who unite with them will by their ministers be received into their church by rebaptism and repentance and newness of life. They henceforth lead their lives under a semblance of a quite spiritual conduct. They denounce covetousness, pride, profanity, the lewd conversation and immorality of the world, drinking and gluttony. In short, their hypocrisy is great and manifold.[31]

Bullinger's lament (1531) that "the people are

running after them as though they were the living saints" has been reported earlier. Vadian, the reformer of St. Gall, testified, that "none were more favorably inclined toward Anabaptism and more easily entangled with it than those who were of pious and honorable disposition."[32] Capito, the reformer of Strassburg, wrote in 1527 concerning the Swiss Brethren:

I frankly confess that in most [Anabaptists] there is in evidence piety and consecration and indeed a zeal which is beyond any suspicion of insincerity. For what earthly advantage could they hope to win by enduring exile, torture, and unspeakable punishment of the flesh? I testify before God that I cannot say that on account of a lack of wisdom they are somewhat indifferent toward earthly things, but rather from divine motives.[33]

The preachers of the Canton of Berne admitted in a letter to the Council of Berne in 1532 that

The Anabaptists have the semblance of outward piety to a far greater degree than we and all the churches which unitedly with us confess Christ, and they avoid offensive sins which are very common among us.[34]

Walter Klarer, the Reformed chronicler of Appenzell, Switzerland, wrote:

Most of the Anabaptists are people who at first had been the best with us in promulgating the word of God.[35]

And the Roman Catholic theologian, Franz Agricola, in his book of 1582, *Against the Terrible Errors of the Anabaptists,* says:

Among the existing heretical sects there is none which in appearance leads a more modest or pious life than the Anabaptist. As concerns their outward public life they are irreproachable. No lying, deception, swearing, strife, harsh language, no intemperate eating and drinking, no outward personal display, is found among them, but humility, patience, uprightness, neatness, honesty, temperance, straightforwardness in such measure that one would suppose that they had the Holy Spirit of God.[36]

A mandate against the Swiss Brethren published in 1585 by the Council of Berne states that offensive sins and vices were common among the preachers and the membership of the Reformed Church, adding, "And this is the greatest reason that many pious, God-fearing people who seek Christ from their heart are offended and forsake our church [to unite with the Brethren]."[37]

One of the finest contemporary characterizations of the Anabaptists is that given in 1531 by Sebastian Franck, an objective and sympathetic witness, though an opponent of the Anabaptists, who wrote as follows:

The Anabaptists . . . soon gained a large following, . . . drawing many sincere souls who had a zeal for God, for they taught nothing but love, faith, and the cross. They showed themselves humble, patient under much suffering; they brake bread with one another as an evidence of unity and love. They helped each other faithfully, and called each other brothers. . . . They died as martyrs, patiently and humbly enduring all persecution.[38]

A further confirmation of the above evaluation of the achievement of the Anabaptists is found in the fact that in many places those who lived a consistent Christian life were in danger of falling under the suspicion of being guilty of Anabaptist heresy. Caspar Schwenckfeld, for instance, declared, "I am being maligned, by both preachers and others, with the charge of being Anabaptist, even as all others who lead a true, pious Christian life are now almost everywhere given this name."[39] Bullinger himself complained that

. . . there are those who in reality are not Anabaptists but have a pronounced averseness to the sensuality and frivolity of the world and therefore reprove sin and vice and are consequently called or misnamed Anabaptists by petulant persons.[40]

The great collection of Anabaptist source materials, commonly called the *Täufer-Akten,* now in its third volume, contains a number of specific illustrations of this. In 1562 a certain

Caspar Zacher of Wailblingen in Württemberg was accused of being an Anabaptist, but the court record reports that since he was an envious man who could not get along with others, and who often started quarrels, as well as being guilty of swearing and cursing and carrying a weapon, he was not considered to be an Anabaptist.[41] On the other hand in 1570 a certain Hans Jäger of Vöhringen in Württemberg was brought before the court on suspicion of being an Anabaptist primarily because he did not curse but lived an irreproachable life.[42]

As a second major element in the Anabaptist vision, a new concept of the church was created by the central principle of newness of life and applied Christianity. Voluntary church membership based upon true conversion and involving a commitment to holy living and discipleship was the absolutely essential heart of this concept. This vision stands in sharp contrast to the church concept of the reformers who retained the medieval idea of a mass church with membership of the entire population from birth to the grave compulsory by law and force.

It is from the standpoint of this new conception of the church that the Anabaptist opposition to infant baptism must be interpreted. Infant baptism was not the cause of their disavowal of the state church; it was only a symbol of the cause. How could infants give a commitment based upon a knowledge of what true Christianity means? They might conceivably passively experience the grace of God (though Anabaptists would question this), but they could not respond in pledging their lives to Christ. Such infant baptism would not only be meaningless, but would in fact become a serious obstacle to a true understanding of the nature of Christianity and membership in the church. Only adult baptism could signify an intelligent life commitment.

An inevitable corollary of the concept of the church as a body of committed and practicing Christians pledged to the highest standard of New Testament living was the insistence on the separation of the church from the world, that is nonconformity of the Christian to the worldly way of life. The world would not tolerate the practice of true Christian principles in society, and the church could not tolerate the practice of worldly ways among its membership. Hence, the only way out was separation (*"Absonderung"*), the gathering of true Christians into their own Christian society where Christ's way could and would be practiced. On this principle of separation Menno Simons says:

All the evangelical scriptures teach us that the church of Christ was and is, in doctrine, life, and worship, a people separated from the world.[43]

In the great debate of 1528 at Zofingen, spokesmen of the Swiss Brethren said:

The true church is separated from the world and is conformed to the nature of Christ. If a church is yet at one with the world we cannot recognize it is a true church. [44]

In a sense, this principle of nonconformity to the world is merely a negative expression of the positive requirement of discipleship, but it goes further in the sense that it represents a judgment on the contemporary social order, which the Anabaptists called "the world," as non-Christian, and sets up a line of demarcation between the Christian community and worldly society.

A logical outcome of the concept of nonconformity to the world was the concept of the suffering church. Conflict with the world was inevitable for those who endeavored to live an earnest Christian life. The Anabaptists expected opposition; they took literally the words of Jesus when He said, "In the world ye shall have tribulation," but they also took literally His words of encouragement, "But be of good cheer; I have overcome the world." Conrad Grebel said in 1524:

True Christian believers are sheep among wolves, sheep for the slaughter; they must be baptized in anguish and affliction, tribulation, persecution, suffering, and death; they must be tried with fire and must reach the fatherland of eternal rest not by killing their bodily, but by mortifying their spiritual, enemies. [45]

Professor Ernest Staehelin of Basel, Switzerland, says:

Anabaptism by its earnest determination to follow in life and practice the primitive Christian Church has kept alive the conviction that he who is in Christ is a new creature and that those who are identified with his cause will necessarily encounter the opposition of the world.[46]

Perhaps it was persecution that made the Anabaptists so acutely aware of the conflict between the church and the world, but this persecution was due to the fact that they refused to accept what they considered the sub-Christian way of life practiced in European Christendom. They could have avoided the persecution had they but conformed, or they could have suspended the practice of their faith to a more convenient time and sailed under false colors as did David Joris, but they chose with dauntless courage and simple honesty to live their faith, to defy the existing world order, and to suffer the consequences.

Basic to the Anabaptist vision of the church was the insistence on the practice of true brotherhood and love among the members of the church.[47] This principle was understood to mean not merely the expression of pious sentiments, but the actual practice of sharing possessions to meet the needs of others in the spirit of true mutual aid. Hans Leopold, a Swiss Brethren martyr of 1528, said of the Brethren:

If they know of any one who is in need, whether or not he is a member of their church, they believe it their duty, out of love to God, to render help and aid.[48]

Heinrich Seiler, a Swiss Brethren martyr of 1535, said:

I do not believe it wrong that a Christian has property of his own, but yet he is nothing more than a steward.[49]

An early Hutterian book states that one of the questions addressed by the Swiss Brethren to applicants for baptism was: "Whether they would consecrate themselves with all their temporal possessions to the service of God and His people."[50] A Protestant of Strassburg, visitor at a Swiss Brethren baptismal service in that city in 1557, reports that a question addressed to all applicants for baptism was: "Whether they, if necessity require it, would devote all their possessions to the service of the brotherhood, and would not fail any member that is in need, if they were able to render aid."[51] Heinrich Bullinger, the bitter enemy of the Brethren, states:

They teach that every Christian is under duty before God from motives of love, to use, if need be, all his possessions to supply the necessities of life to any of the brethren who are in need.[52]

This principle of full brotherhood and steward-ship was actually practiced, and not merely speculatively considered. In its absolute form of Christian communism, with the complete repudiation of private property, it became the way of life of the Hutterian Brotherhood in 1528 and has remained so to this day, for the Hutterites held that private property is the greatest enemy of Christian love. One of the inspiring stories of the sixteenth and seventeenth centuries is the successful practice of the full communal way of life by this group.[53]

The third great element in the Anabaptist vision was the ethic of love and nonresistance as applied to all human relationships. The Brethren understood this to mean complete abandonment of all warfare, strife, and vio-lence, and of the taking of human life.[54] Con-rad Grebel, the Swiss, said in 1524:

True Christians use neither worldly sword nor engage in war, since among them taking human life has ceased entirely, for we are no longer under the Old Covenant. . . . The Gospel and those who accept it are not to be protected with the sword, neither should they thus protect them-selves.[55]

Pilgram Marpeck, the South German leader, in 1544, speaking of Matthew 5, said:

All bodily, worldly, carnal, earthly fightings, conflicts, and wars are annulled and abolished among them through such law . . . which law of love Christ . . . Himself observed and thereby gave His followers a pattern to follow after.[56]

Peter Riedemann, the Hutterian leader, wrote in 1545:

Christ, the Prince of Peace, has established His Kingdom, that is, His Church, and has purchased it by His blood. In this kingdom all worldly warfare has ended. Therefore a Christian has no part in war nor does he wield the sword to execute vengeance.[57]

Menno Simons, of Holland, wrote in 1550:

The regenerated do not go to war, nor engage in strife. . . . They are the children of peace who have beaten their swords into plowshares and their spears into pruning hooks, and know of no war. . . . Spears and swords of iron we leave to those who, alas, consider human blood and swine's blood of well-nigh equal value.[58]

In this principle of nonresistance, or biblical pacifism, which was thoroughly believed and resolutely practiced by all the original Anabaptist Brethren and their descendants throughout Europe from the beginning until the last century,[59] the Anabaptists were again creative leaders, far ahead of their times, in this antedating the Quakers by over a century and a

32

quarter. It should also be remembered that they held this principle in a day when both Catholic and Protestant churches not only endorsed war as an instrument of state policy, but employed it in religious conflicts. It is true, of course, that occasional earlier prophets, like Peter Chelcicky, had advocated similar views, but they left no continuing practice of the principle behind them.

As we review the vision of the Anabaptists, it becomes clear that there are two foci in this vision. The first focus relates to the essential nature of Christianity. Is Christianity primarily a matter of the reception of divine grace through a sacramental-sacerdotal institution (Roman Catholicism), is it chiefly enjoyment of the inner experience of the grace of God through faith in Christ (Lutheranism), or is it most of all the transformation of life through discipleship (Anabaptism)? The Anabaptists were neither institutionalists, mystics, nor pietists, for they laid the weight of their emphasis upon following Christ in life. To them it was unthinkable for one truly to be a Christian without creating a new life on divine principles both for himself and for all men who commit themselves to the Christian way.

The second focus relates to the church. For the Anabaptist, the church was neither an institution (Catholicism), nor the instrument of God for the proclamation of the divine Word

(Lutheranism), nor a resource group for individual piety (Pietism). It was a brotherhood of love in which the fullness of the Christian life ideal is to be expressed.

The Anabaptist vision may be further clarified by comparison of the social ethics of the four main Christian groups of the Reformation period, Catholic, Calvinist, Lutheran, and Anabaptist. Catholic and Calvinist alike were optimistic about the world, agreeing that the world can be redeemed; they held that the entire social order can be brought under the sovereignty of God and Christianized, although they used different means to attain this goal. Lutheran and Anabaptist were pessimistic about the world, denying the possibility of Christianizing the entire social order; but the consequent attitudes of these two groups toward the social order were diametrically opposed. Lutheranism said that since the Christian must live in a world order that remains sinful, he must make a compromise with it. As a citizen he cannot avoid participation in the evil of the world, for instance in making war, and for this his only recourse is to seek forgiveness by the grace of God; only within his personal private experience can the Christian truly Christianize his life. The Anabaptist rejected this view completely. Since for him no compromise dare be made with evil, the Christian may in no circumstance participate in any conduct in the existing social order which is contrary to the spirit and teaching of Christ and the apostolic practice. He must consequently withdraw from the worldly system and create a Christian social order within the fellowship of the church brotherhood. Extension of this Christian order by the conversion of individuals and their transfer out of the world into the church is the only way by which progress can be made in Christianizing the social order.

However, the Anabaptist was realistic. Down the long perspective of the future he saw little chance that the mass of humankind would enter such a brotherhood with its high ideals. Hence he anticipated a long and grievous conflict between the church and the world. Neither did he anticipate the time when the church would rule the world; the church would always be a suffering church. He agreed with the words of Jesus when He said that those who would be His disciples must deny themselves and take up their cross daily and follow Him, and that there would be few who would enter the strait gate and travel the narrow way of life. If this prospect should seem too discouraging, the Anabaptist would reply that the life within the Christian brotherhood is satisfyingly full of love and joy.

The Anabaptist vision was not a detailed blueprint for the reconstruction of human society, but the Brethren did believe that Jesus intended that the kingdom of God should be set up in the midst of earth, here and now, and this they proposed to do forthwith. We shall not believe, they said, that the Sermon on the Mount or any other vision that He had is only a heavenly vision meant but to keep His followers in tension until the last great day, but we shall practice what He taught, believing that where He walked we can by His grace follow in His steps.

FOOTNOTES

1 Reprinted from *Church History* (March 1944) XIII, 3-24, with slight revisions.

2 Rufus M. Jones, *Studies in Mystical Religion* (London, 1909) 369.

Professor Walter Köhler of Heidelberg has recently expressed a similar evaluation, asserting that the historical significance of the Anabaptists "erschöpft sich nicht in dem Duldermut, der Arbeitstreue, dem kulturellen Fleiss. . . . Nein, die Mennoniten dürfen ohne Uberhebung einen Platz in der Weltgeschichte beanspruchen als Bahnbrecher der modernen Weltanschauung mit ihrer Glaubens — und Gewissensfreiheit."

3 The results of this research are best found in: *Mennonitisches Lexikon,* edited by Christian Hege and Christian Neff (Frankfurt a. M. and Weierhof [Pfalz], Germany, 1913 ff.), now at the letter "N"; Ernst Correll, *Das Schweizerishe Täufermennonitentum: Ein Soziologischer Bericht* (Tübingen, 1925); *Mennonite Quarterly Review* (published at Goshen, Indiana, since 1927); *Mennonitische Geschichtsblätter* (published at Weierhof [Palatinate] since 1936); R. J. Smithson, *The Anabaptists, Their Contribution to Our Protestant Heritage* (London, 1935); John Horsch, *Mennonites in Europe* (Scottdale, Pa., 1942); C. Henry Smith, *The Story of the Mennonites* (Berne, Indiana, 1941); L. von Muralt, *Glaube und Lehre der Schweizerschen Wiedertäufer in der Reformationszeit* (Zurich, 1938). Cf. also: Wilhelm Pauck "The Historiography of the German Reformation During the Past Twenty Years; IV. Research in the History of the Anabaptists," *Church History* (December 1940) IX, 335-364; Harold S. Bender, "Recent Progress in Research in Anabaptist History," *Mennonite Quarterly Review* (January 1934) VIII, 3-17. Only three volumes of the great source publication, *Quellen zur Geschichte der Wiedertäufer* (Leipzig, 1930 ff.), published by the *Verein fur Reformationsgeschichte,* have yet appeared.

4. Quoted in translation by John Horsch, *Mennonites in Europe,* 325, from Bullinger's *Der Wiedertäufferen Ursprung,* etc., Zurich, 1560.

5 Horsch, 293, from Sebastian Frank's *Chronica, Zeitbuch und Geschichtbibel* (Strassburg, 1531).

6 Heinrich Bullinger, *Von dem unverschampten fräfel . . . der selvsgesandten Widertouffern* (Zurich, 1531), folio 2v.

7 F. Roth, *Augsburgs Reformationsgeschichte* (Munich, 1901), I, 230.

8 Letter of Zwingli to Vadian, May 28, 1525, *Huldreich Zwinglis Sämtliche Werke* ed. Egli, Finsler, Köhler, *et al.* (Leipzig, 1914) VII, 332.

9 The full official text of the decree may be found in *Aller des Heiligen Roemischen Reichs gehaltene Reichstage, Abschiede und Satzungen* (Mainz, 1666), 210, 211. It is also edited by Ludwig Keller in *Monatshefte der Comenius Gesellschaft* (Berlin, 1900), IX, 55-57, and by Bossert in "Die Reichsgesetze über die Wiedertäufer" in *Quellen zur Geschichte der Wiedertäufer, I. Band Herzogtum Württemberg* (Leipzig, 1930), 1°-10°. See the excellent discussion of Anabaptist persecution by John Horsch in "The Persecution of the Evangelical Anabaptists," *Mennonite Quarterly Review* (January 1938), XII, 3-26.

10 *Geschicht-Buch der Hutterischen Brüder*, edited by Rudolf Wolkan (Macleod [Alberta] and Vienna, 1923), 142, 181.

11 *Ibid.*, 182-187. The following quotation is composed of extracts selected from this account without regard to the original order, chiefly from 186, 187.

12 *Gottfried Keller's Werke,* ed. by Max Nussberger (Leipzig, n. d.) VI, 309. See Elizabeth Horsch Bender, "The Portrayal of the Swiss Anabaptists in Gottfried Keller's Ursula," *Mennonite Quarterly Review* [July, 1943] XVII, 136-150.

13 In Switzerland, this group was called "Swiss Brethren," in Austria "Hutterites," in Holland and North Germany, "Menists." All these groups seriously objected to the name "Anabaptists" which was a term used to designate a punishable heresy and which after the tragic Münster episode (1534-35) was a name of odious opprobrium. I use the term here only for custom's sake. The term "Mennonite" came into wider use in the seventeenth century and was ultimately applied to all the groups except the Hutterites.

14 Ernst H. Correll, *Das Schweizerische Täufermennonitentum* (Tübingen, 1925), "Allgemeine historisch-soziologische Kennzeichnung," 3-10, gives an excellent concise survey. See particularly 6, footnote 1. See also Karl Kautsky, *Communism in Central Europe in the Time of the Reformation* (1897). Troeltsch rejected the theory of the socioeconomic origin of the Anabaptists.

15 Albrecht Ritschl, *Geshichte des Pietismus* (Bonn, 1880). Cf. R. Friedmann, "Conception of the Anabaptist," *Church History* (December 1940) IX, 351.

16 Ludwig Keller, *Die Reformation und die älteren Reformparteien* (Leipzig, 1885). Cf. also Friedmann, *op. cit.*, 352.

17 Max Göbel, *Geschichte des Christlichen Lebens*, etc. (Coblentz, 1848), I, 134. Ritschl, *op. cit.*, 22, characterizes Göbel's

views as follows: "Die Wiedertäuferei also soll nach Göbel die gründlichere, entschiedenere, vollständigere Reformation sein, welche als 'Kind der Reformation' Luthers und Zwinglis zu erkennen aber von Luther seit 1522, von Zwingli seit 1524 aufgegeben worden wäre." Ritschl (*op. cit.*, 7) himself states the Anabaptist position as follows: "Nicht minder haben die Wiedertäufer sich dafur angesehen, dass sie das von Luther und Zwingli begonnene Werk der Wiederherstellung der Kirche zu seinem rechten Ziel führten."

18 Horsch, *op. cit.*, 289.

19 Letter of Conrad Grebel to Thomas Müntzer, Sept. 5, 1524, *Thomas Müntzers Briefwechsel*, ed. H. Böhmer, and P. Kirn (Leipzig, 1931), 92; English translation, Walter Rauschenbusch, "The Zurich Anabaptists and Thomas Münzer." *American Journal of Theology* (January 1905) IX, 92.

20 Taken from an unpublished manuscript in the *Staatsarchiv des Kantons Bern, (Unnütze Papiere, Bd.* 80), entitled *Acta des Gesprächs zwüschenn predicannten und Touffbrüderenn* (1538), Copy in the Goshen College Library.

21 Karl Holl, *Gesammelte Aufsätze zur Kirchengeschichte* (2nd and 3rd ed.) (Tübingen, 1923), 359.

22 *Corpus Schwenckfeldianorum* (Leipzig, 1911), II, 280 f. See also K. Ecke, *Schwenckfeld, Luther und der Gedanke einer apostolischen Reformation* (Berlin, 1911), 101 f. See also the discussion on this topic in J. Horsch, "The Rise of State Church Protestantism," *Mennonite Quarterly Review* (July 1932), VI, 189-191.

22a See Luther's *Deutsche Messe*, translated in *Works of Martin Luther* (ed. C. M. Jacobs *et al.)* Vol. VI (Philadelphia, 1932), 172, 173.

23 "Drei Zeugenaussagen Zwinglis im Täuferprozess" in *Huldreich Zwinglis Sämtliche Werke* (Leipzig, 1927), IV, 169.

24 Against this interpretation of Luther (and Zwingli) it may be argued that Luther never completely and consistently adopted the concept of a church of "earnest Christians only" which is here attributed to him, but that along with it he also retained the contradictory concept of the church functioning as a "corpus regens," that is, as an institution of social control. It may be agreed that Luther held the two concepts for a time and that he finally abandoned the former in favor of the latter, but the fact nevertheless remains that the former was for a time dominant, and that it is the implicit meaning of his whole basic theological position. The retention and eventual dominance of the second concept is an evidence of the carry-over of medievalism in Luther's thought. In regard to Zwingli, Wilhelm Hadorn says: "It must be admitted that not only Zwingli but also other Swiss and South

German Reformers, e.g., Oecolampad and Capito, originally held views similar to the Anabaptists" (Die Reformation in der Deutschen Schweiz. [Leipzig, 1928]. 104). Walter Köhler, the best living authority on Zwingli, says; "Es ist, wie bei Luther auch, die Kapitulation der autonomen kirchgemeinschaft vor der Obrigkeit eingetreten." (*Zwinglis Werke* [Leipzig, 1927], IV, 29).

25 Karl Müller, *Kirchengeschichte*, II, I, 476, Müller describes the essential goal of the Anabaptists as follows: "Es bedeutete inmitten der Auflösung aller Verhältnisse genug, dass hier eine Gemeinschaft stand, die die Heiligung des Lebens allem anderen voranstellte und zugleich in dem unteren Volksschichten wirklich Fuss gefasst, sie mit selbständiger Religiöstät gefüllt hat." (Kirchengeschichte, II, 1, 330.)

26 Johannes Kühn, *Toleranz und Offenbarung* (Leipzig, 1923), 224 says: "With the Anabaptists everything was based on a central idea. This central idea was concretely religious. It was Jesus' command to follow Him in a holy life of fellowship." Professor Alfred Hegler of Tübingen describes the Anabaptist ideal as "liberty of conscience, rejection of all state-made Christianity, the demand for personal holiness, and a vital personal acceptance of Christian truth." Professor Paul Wernle says, "Their vital characteristic was the earnestness with which they undertook the practical fulfillment of New Testament requirements both for the individual and for the church." These and other similar quotations are to be found in Horsch. "The Character of the Evangelical Anabaptists as Reported by Contemporary Reformation Writers." *Mennonite Quarterly Review* (July 1934), VIII, 135.

27 Pilgrim Marpeck, the outstanding writer of the Swiss and South German Brethren, is an example. See J. C. Wenger, "The Theology of Pilgrim Marpeck," *Mennonite Quarterly Review* (October 1938), XII, 247.

28 The German (Luther) translation of 1 Peter 3:21 calls baptism "Der Bund eines guten Gewissens mit Gott."

29 Bullinger, *Von dem unverschampten fräfel* (1531), fol. 75 r.

30 S. M. Jackson, *Selected Works of Huldreich Zwingli* (Philadelphia, 1901), 127.

31 Bullinger, *Der Widertäufferen Ursprung*, fol. 15 v.

32 Joachim von Watt, *Deutsche Historische Schriften*, ed. Ernst Götzinger (St. Gall, 1879), II, 408.

33 C. A. Cornelius, *Geschichte des Münsterschen Aufruhrs* (Leipzig, 1860), II, 52.

34 W. J. McGlothlin, *Die Berner Täufer bis 1532* (berlin, 1902), 36.

35 J. J. Simler, *Sammlung alter und neuer Urkunden* (Zurich, 1757), I, 824.

36 Karl Rembert, *Die Wiedertäufer im Herzogtum Jülich* (Berlin, 1899), 564.

37 Ernst Müller, *Geschichte der Bernischen Täufer* (Frauenfeld, 1895), 88. Müller speaks (p. 89) of the mandate of 1585 as conceiving of "das Täuferwesen" as a just judgment of God on the church and the people of Berne.

38 Sebastian Franck, *Chronica, Zeitbuch und Geschichtbibel* (Strassburg, 1531), folio 444v.

39 Schwenckfeld's *Epistolar* (1564), I, 203.

40 Bullinger, *Der Widertäufferen Ursprung* (1561), fol. 170r.

41 *Quellen zur Geschichte der Wiedertäufer, I. Band Herzogtum Württemberg*, ed. Gustav Bossert (Leipzig, 1930), 216 f.

42 *Ibid.*, 259 ff.

43 *Complete Works of Menno Simons* (Elkhart, Indiana, 1871), II, 37b.

44 *Handlung oder Acta der Disputation gehalten zu Zofingen* (Zurich, 1532).

45 Böhmer-Kirn, *op. cit.*, 97.

46 Horsch, *op cit.*, 386.

47 P. Tschackert, *Die Entstehung der Lutherischen und reformierten Kirchenlehre* (Göttingen, 1910), 133, says of the Anabaptists that they were "a voluntary Christian fellowship, striving to conform to the Christian spirit for the practice of brotherly love."

48 Johannes Kühn, *op. cit.*, 231. fol. 22v.

49 Ernst Müller, *op. cit.*, 44. See Ernst Correll, *op. cit.*, 15 f. on the attitude of the various Anabaptist groups on community of goods.

50 Horsch, *op. cit.*, 317.

51 A. Hulshof *Geschiedenis van de Doopsgezinden te Straatsburg van 1525 tot 1557* (Amsterdam, 1905), 216.

52 Bullinger, *Der Widertäufferen Ursprung*, fol. 129v.

53 John Horsch, *The Hutterian Brethren 1528-1931* (Goshen, Indiana, 1931), gives the only adequate account in English of the Hutterian Brethren. It is of interest to note that Erasmus, Melanchthon, and Zwingli condemned private ownership of property as a sin. See Paul Wernle, *Renaissance und Reformation* (Tübingen, 1912), 54, 55, for the citations of Erasmus and Melanchthon, and Horsch, *Hutterian Brethren*, 132, footnote 126, for the citation of Zwingli. Wilhelm Pauck says that Bucer's ideal state was that of Christian communism, "Martin Bucer's Conception of a Christian State," in *Princeton Theological Review* (January 1928), XXVI, 88.

54 Not all the Anabaptists were completely nonresistant. Balthasar Hubmaier for instance for a brief period (1526-28) led a group of Anabaptists at Nikolsburg in Moravia who agreed to carry the

sword against the Turk and pay special war taxes for this purpose. This group, which became extinct in a short time, was known as the "Schwertler" in distinction from other Moravian Anabaptists called the "Stäbler," who later became the Hutterites and have continued to the present. It is obvious that Hubmaier and the "Schwertler" represent a transient aberration from original and authentic Anabaptism. Bullinger (*Von dem unverschampten fräfel* [1531] fol. 139v.) testifies that the Swiss Brethren considered war to be "das ergist uebel das man erdencken mag," and (*Der Widertäufferen Ursprung* [1561] fol. 16 r.) says "they do not defend themselves, therefore they do not go to war and are not obedient to the government on this point." See also, extensive compilation of evidence by John Horsch in his booklet, *The Principle of Nonresistance as Held by the Mennonite Church, A Historical Survey* (Scottdale, Pa., 1927), 60 pages.

55 Letter of Grebel to Müntzer, Böhmer-Kirn, *op. cit.,* 97.

56 (Pilgrim Marpeck), *Testamenterleütterung* (n.d., n.p., ca. 1544), fol. 313r.

57 (Peter Riedemann), *Rechenschaft unserer Religion, Lehre und Glaubens, von den Bruedern die Man die Hutterischen nennt* (Berne, Indiana, 1902), 105.

58 *The Complete Works of Menno Simons* (Elkhart, Indiana, 1871), I, 170b and 81b. The quotations were revised by comparison with the Dutch editions of 1664 and 1681.

59 Mennonites of Holland, Germany, France, and Switzerland gradually abandoned nonresistance in the course of the nineteenth century. The emigrant Mennonites in Russia and North America have maintained it. The Mennonites of the United States furnish 40 percent of all conscientious objectors in Civilian Public Service in the present war, and the Mennonites of Canada a still higher percent of the conscientious objectors in that country.

THE AUTHOR

Harold S. Bender was born July 19, 1897, at Elkhart, Indiana. He held degrees from the following institutions: BS, Goshen College, Goshen, Indiana; BD, Garrett Biblical Institute; ThM, Princeton Theological Seminary; MA, Princeton University; and ThD, Heidelberg University.

He became dean of Goshen College in 1933 and from 1944 he served as dean of Goshen College Biblical Seminary until his death, September 21, 1962.

In the Mennonite Church he was active in many organizations and committees most notable as chair-

43

man of the Historical and Research Committee and the Peace Problems Committee. He was ordained to the ministry June 18, 1944. He became president of the Mennonite World Conference in 1952 and served until his death.

In 1927 he founded the scholarly quarterly, *The Mennonite Quarterly Review*, and served as its editor until his death. He served as editor of *The Mennonite Encyclopedia*, a four-volume monumental contribution to Christendom. In addition to numerous articles in various scholarly magazines he was also author of *Two Centuries of American Mennonite Literature: Conrad Grebel, First Leader of the Swiss Brethren; These Are My People; Mennonite Origins in Europe;* and *Biblical Revelation and Inspiration.*

The Anabaptist Vision, given as a presidential address before the American Society of Church History in 1942, has become a classic essay. Since its delivery it has appeared in scholarly journals and translated into several languages.